WHAT HAPPENED?: THE MICHAELS ABROAD

Conversations in Angers, France

Part Two of The Michaels

Richard Nelson

BROADWAY PLAY PUBLISHING INC
New York
www.broadwayplaypub.com
info@broadwayplaypub.com

WHAT HAPPENED?: THE MICHAELS ABROAD

First edition: October 2021
I S B N: 978-0-88145-915-9

Book design: Marie Donovan
Page make-up: Adobe InDesign
Typeface: Palatino

WHAT HAPPENED?: THE MICHAELS ABROAD: was produced by Hunter Theater Project (Gregory Mosher, Producer) in An Independent Theater production, opening on 8 September 2021. The cast and creative contributors were:

KATE HARRIS .... Maryann Plunkett
DAVID MICHAEL .... Jay O Sanders
SALLY MICHAEL .... Rita Wolf
LUCY MICHAEL .... Charlotte Bydwell
IRENIE WALKER .... Haviland Morris
MAY SMITH .... Matilda Sakamoto
SUZANNE RAPHAEL .... Yvonne Woods

Director .... Richard Nelson
Scenic Designer .... Jason Ardizzonne-West
Costume Designer .... Susan Hilferty
Lighting Designer .... Jennifer Tipton
Sound Designer .... Will Pickens
Dances based on original choreography .... Dan Wagoner
Choreography Consultant .... Gwyneth Jones
Production Stage Manager .... Theresa Flanagan
Stage Manager .... Jared Oberholtzer
Press Representative .... Candi Adams
General management .... Martin Platt, Tim Smith
Production Manager .... Jeff Harris
Production Assistant .... Hailey Delany

CHARACTERS

Mentioned in the play:

Rose Michael (1952-2021), choreographer, dancer, founder and former artistic director of The Rose Michael Dance Company.

In the play:

KATE HARRIS, *68, retired history teacher; Rose's widow.*

DAVID MICHAEL, *69, Rose's ex-husband; arts manager and producer; former manager of Rose's dance company.*

SALLY MICHAEL *62,* DAVID*'s wife, and former principal dancer with Rose's company.*

LUCY MICHAEL, *33, Rose and* DAVID*'s daughter; a dancer, choreographer; had been on a six-month residency at the Centre National de Danse Contemporaire (C N D C) in Angers, France, which turned into one of a year and nine months.*

MAY SMITH, *26, Rose's niece (her sister's daughter); dancer; she has been staying with* LUCY *and* SUZANNE *in Angers for the past two months.*

IRENIE WALKER, *60, former principal dancer with Rose's company. On leave as an administrator at Gibney Studios downtown, recently arrived in Europe. Lives in Manhattan.*

SUZANNE RAPHAEL, *46, former dancer with the Rose Michael Company in New York, now a part-time instructor at the C N D C-Angers.*

Also mentioned in the play:

Jacques Francois Raphael, 52, SUZANNE*'s older brother; former principal dancer with the Rose Michael Company in New York; instructor at the C N D C-Angers; lives in Angers with his new wife, Maria.*

SETTING

SUZANNE RAPHAEL's *apartment, Angers, France, which she shared with her brother for many years; approximately two hours west of Paris by train.*

The three-bedroom apartment is on the second floor of a building on the rue Saint Jacques, about a twenty-five-minute walk from the train station, and a five-minute walk from The Quai, home of the C N D C-Angers.

The kitchen area.

Time: Wednesday, September 8, 2021. 5:30pm to approximately 8:30pm.

The meal:

During the first four scenes, an Italian meal is prepared by SUZANNE, *with the help of* LUCY *and* MAY. (DAVID *and* SALLY *will also help,)*

Lasagna, fresh bread, various antipasto, cheeses, wine, cider and water.

NOTE ON THE DANCES

The original production of WHAT HAPPENED?: THE MICHAELS ABROAD incorporated and adapted dances made in the 1980s and 1990s by the choreographer Dan Wagoner for his company The Dan Wagoner Dancers. For subsequent productions, other, appropriate, dances may be substituted.

AUTHOR'S NOTE

I use a single quotation mark to notate when the character is paraphrasing, and double quotation marks when the character is actually reading from a source.

NOTE ON MUSIC

"Nothing is more real than nothing."
—Samuel Beckett

For Susie & Gregory

(Furniture: chairs and benches, stool, worktable, dinner table and small square table; rugs, stove, sink, cabinet, small garbage can.)

(In the dark, Katie Herzig's Lost And Found *plays through the main speakers.)*

(Actors enter with props to arrange and create the area in SUZANNE RAPHAEL'*s kitchen: bowls of vegetables, cutting boards, cookbooks, etc. [The refrigerator is unseen and just 'off' in the pantry.])*

(Two entrances: one from the pantry, and the other from the rest of the apartment [bedrooms, living room, stairwell to the outside].)

(5:30 P M)

(Wednesday, September 8, 2021.)

1.
Young Rose.

(Bread is baking in the oven.)

*(*SUZANNE *with* MAY'*s help is working on the lasagna.* SUZANNE *is cutting cauliflower.)*

*(*LUCY *and* DAVID *have stopped their work on the antipasto.)*

(Timer ticks on the oven.)

*(*DAVID *has a shoebox full of old letters.)*

(In the middle of a conversation:)

DAVID: One day Kate got your Mom talking. I don't know how she did that, but she did. We're sitting in Kate's garden, at least ten feet away from each other. Kate had very strict rules. *(Obviously)* Masked… And Rose says to me, about me… She says: "David, you've got something that no one could ever guess just by looking at you, or listening to you." *(Then)* I don't know if this is going to be a joke…

LUCY: I've been there.

DAVID: Your Mom says, "You have an acceptance of life and everything it brings. Most people quarrel with it, rebel against it. But for you, David—life is a gift."

LUCY: I think you can seem like that sometimes. I can understand Mom seeing you that way.

DAVID: I'd like to be like that. I wish I were like that… And she said something about you, Lucy…

LUCY: What?

DAVID: She'd read this somewhere. It reminded her of you, she said. Of you being always so 'confident'.

LUCY: *(Turns to* SUZANNE*)* If she'd seen me here.

SUZANNE: Not true.

DAVID: About a little girl in school making a drawing. The teacher comes by and asks what she's making. The girl explains, 'I'm drawing a picture of God.' The teacher smiles, nods, and says, 'you know, people don't know what God looks like.' The little girl looks up at the teacher and says, 'Now they will.' *(Smiles)*

LUCY: That sounds more like Mom.

MAY: *(To* LUCY*)* Maybe both of you.

DAVID: *(To* MAY*)* I agree. *(To* LUCY*)* It's what she said…

LUCY: She just liked the joke.

DAVID: *(With a letter)* This letter is when your mother was pregnant with you, Lucy… *(Explains)* Suzanne, 1988. Two months before *(*LUCY*)* she's born. Rose is writing about getting back to work. *(To* LUCY*)* She writes about *her* Mom.

MAY: *(To* LUCY*)* Grandma.

DAVID: *(Reads)* "Mom keeps saying that if I love my baby I'll stay with her…"

MAY: And stop dancing?

DAVID: I think that's what your Grandma was saying to her, May. *(Reads)* "That's when I yelled at Mom, as I mentioned when you called on Monday…" I'm obviously away somewhere.

SUZANNE: Hence the letter.

MAY: *(To* LUCY*)* Grandma wanted her to stop dancing and take care of you.

LUCY: I didn't know.

DAVID: *(Another letter)* A really early one. Maybe the earliest, Lucy… She makes little drawings on the side… *(Points out)* She was a good drawer.

LUCY: Can I…?

DAVID: *(Reads)* "Dearest Dave…"

MAY: 'Dave'?

DAVID: *(As he hands the letter to* LUCY*)* Didn't last long, May.

SUZANNE: Read it out loud.

LUCY: *(Reads)* "Dearest Dave… It's Monday morning and I am inspired to write you…"

DAVID: 'Inspired.' She's making fun of herself or me. Probably me. Usually me.

SUZANNE: What's the date?

LUCY: *(Reads)* "April 9th, 1973. Monday."

DAVID: May, this was when we had something called 'letters'...

*(*MAY *ignores this.)*

SUZANNE: *(To* LUCY*)* Can I see the envelope?

*(*LUCY *gives* SUZANNE *an envelope.)*

LUCY: *(About the stamp)* From England.

DAVID: We were just married. We were in England.

LUCY: *(Reads)* "I woke up early and it was quite sunny outside. Lying in bed I felt a twinge of bitterness about our snowless winter but then I got up to make a new day...." *(Repeats)* 'Make a new day.' *(Continues)* "But God works in such strange ways, I had to laugh—there was now more snow than we'd seen all winter! And it was this that inspired me to write you."

SUZANNE: Where are you here, David?

DAVID: Salzburg. The first time since getting married that we are away from each other.

LUCY: *(Reads)* "I'll also tell you what I did yesterday. After you left, I did not 'pine away.'" In quotes. "I did my exercises."

DAVID: I'd probably told her not to 'pine away' too much while I was gone. She's just giving it back to me.

SUZANNE: I hear Rose.

LUCY: *(Reads)* "At seven I went out to get the paper, not wanting all those blighty Englishmen to buy them up ahead of me. I *bounded* out of the house..." Sounds so young, Dad. A very different voice than the one I hear in my head...

MAY: Your Mom's not talking to a daughter.

DAVID: *(To* SUZANNE*)* Nineteen here.

SUZANNE: How long were you and Rose in England?

DAVID: Most of one year.

LUCY: *(Reads)* "This morning I found myself waiting eagerly for the mailman, and when he made his presence known at the slot—I marched out, determined that we would get some important mail… And I found your postcard."

DAVID: I'd sent it before I left. *(As an explanation:)* First time away…

LUCY: *(Reads)* "Around 3:30 I went to the park and the sun was out, though it was still cold. I walked all the way over to the farthest section with the little brook, past the heather, and approached the ducks from the opposite end from which we usually come. I had forgotten the bread!" *(She stops.)*

DAVID: What?

LUCY: Mom and I always fed the ducks in our lake…

MAY: She still sometimes did that.

(LUCY is interested.)

LUCY: She did?

MAY: Kate brought her back to the house a couple of times, and the two of them went to the lake and fed ducks. I watched them from the house.

LUCY: *(Reads)* "Happily, however, there were lots of people out to feed them and a good number of dogs to watch, the peacock was out, the rabbits, roosters, the goats and their kids. All excited by the sense of spring and new life. A world opening up again." *(Then)* "I walked home. At six I switched on the news to make sure that your plane hadn't crashed. Instead: Picasso had died."

DAVID: It pulls you up short, doesn't it? Why? We know he died… All of it—my being away, apart, the snow, the ducks, the Spring coming, the death of Picasso—all seem one thing, all entwined…

LUCY: *(Reads)* "I sat down to soak this in. I will miss his presence in the world. I loved his thick and earthy women and their strange faces." *(Turns the letter over, back to the first page. Reads:)* "April 9th, 1973. Monday." *(Continues to read)* "I stayed up reading, feeling the importance of the day. I hoped for a good dream to give me something more to think about. I warmed my pillow by the heater and warmed my nightgown—the green one—."

DAVID: *(To* SUZANNE*)* I remember the nightgown.

LUCY: "I had a somewhat fitful sleep, hearing a bang at one point and suddenly awake, thinking—there is someone in the room."

(Door bell off interrupts and even startles them.)

LUCY: We'll let them in. Dad, I want to keep reading Mom's letters…

DAVID: That's why I brought them, Lucy.

LUCY: Come on, May.

*(*LUCY *and* MAY *hurry off.)*

SUZANNE: How did they get upstairs?

*(*DAVID *is putting the letters away. Church bells from a nearby church.)*

DAVID: I gave Sal the door code. I wrote it down for her this morning before she left…

SUZANNE: Should we go and—?

DAVID: Let's give Lucy a moment with Kate.

SUZANNE: Of course. Right. And where in the world did you ever find all those?

DAVID: We've been cleaning out stuff in Rose's house. They were in a pile of old receipts, junk, in a closet. How they got there...? There are a lot more—.

(SUZANNE sees IRENIE and SALLY enter.)

SUZANNE: Irenie...

IRENIE: Suzanne... The kitchen. Where else?

SUZANNE: *(Over this)* Thanks for coming. I know Lucy really appreciates it.

IRENIE: She just said that.

SUZANNE: *(Over this)* I heard you were very jet lagged. Are you recovered?

IRENIE: It's been a week. I'm adjusted. Hi David.

DAVID: Hi. Suitcases?

IRENIE: *(To DAVID)* They're in the living room, we brought them up. *(To SUZANNE)* Can I wash my hands? Half the train didn't wear masks. Suzanne... You've gotten even younger.

SUZANNE: Hahahaha.

IRENIE: Now you're supposed to say that about me.

SUZANNE: You've always been young. Look how great you look.

DAVID: Where's Kate?

SALLY: With Lucy...

DAVID: Of course.

IRENIE: Where am I staying?

SUZANNE: *(To IRENIE)* You're with me. My room. You need to rest?

IRENIE: No. No. I'm fine.

SALLY: You two roomed together on the road. It'll be like old times.

(KATE *enters with* LUCY *and* MAY.)

DAVID: Kate…

KATE: *(To* SUZANNE*)* Hi. The kitchen…

SALLY: Like at home… We could be in Rhinebeck, Kate.

KATE: I know… *(About* LUCY*)* She looks even more like her mother…

DAVID: Doesn't she.

KATE: And this one *(*MAY*)* —I think she's grown.

MAY: I haven't.

DAVID: Kate—Suzanne…Suzanne, Kate.

SUZANNE: Nice to meet in person. And not on Zoom.

KATE: It is.

SUZANNE: How do you do, Kate. And welcome.

KATE: Thank you. For everything. You've been taking very good care of Lucy all this time. I can see that.

DAVID: Kate…

(DAVID *goes to hug* KATE.)

KATE: I just saw you last week.

DAVID: Welcome to France.

SALLY: *(To* KATE*)* How about some water? You should drink water. And lots of it.

LUCY: I'm getting it. I said the same thing.

KATE: David, the flight was endless.

DAVID: It always feels that way.

KATE: I'd like to change.

SALLY: Of course you do.

LUCY: Kate, your room's by us. We share a bath. Come on, I'll show you.

SALLY: Keep drinking water.

KATE: What time is it?

DAVID: *(A joke)* In Rhinebeck?

LUCY: *(Over this)* Which towels?

SUZANNE: I set them on her bed…

LUCY: Give me your watch, I'll set it…

*(*LUCY *and* KATE *go.)*

(No one knows what to say.)

IRENIE: Rose should be here…

(Lights fade.)

2.
Merce.

(The same, a short time later)

*(*DAVID, SALLY, IRENIE *sit,* SALLY *is looking at a video on her phone.)*

*(*MAY *and* SUZANNE *are back to working on their parts of the meal. Some are drinking cider or will in the scene.)*

SALLY: *(With her phone, to* DAVID*)* This one, it's the Joyce. Cora filmed it from the booth.

DAVID: Cora, of course. She would.

*(*SALLY *watches the video.)*

(Timer goes off.)

DAVID: What is it? Do you know?

IRENIE: Tell him.

SALLY: It's our last performance, David. Our final show.

*(*MAY *goes to the stove.)*

SALLY: *(To* MAY*)* You sure you don't need help?

MAY: I'm good.

SUZANNE: We have our routine down…

IRENIE: I'm sure you do by now…

(MAY *will take the bread out of the oven.)*

IRENIE: Look at that. Smell that.

SUZANNE: May's now our bread-maker…

MAY: I am…. It should cool…

SALLY: *(The video)* This will play on the wall of Rose's exhibit in Paris…

IRENIE: We didn't know that video existed.

DAVID: Rose would never have allowed this. How did—?

SALLY: *(Over this)* Cora must have sneaked it. *(Again:)* She sent it to Suzanne. Rose comes out, in those baggy…

IRENIE: Wrinkled…

SALLY: 'I-don't-give-a-fuck-sweatpants' and plaid lumberjack shirt. I remember her trying on like twenty different lumberjack shirts to get that look… Her curtain call. *(Describes as it happens on the video:)* Rose teases the audience a little… A little wiggle of a foot. Is she going to dance? She's teasing… And then… She dances. By herself… *(She watches.)*

(LUCY *enters.)*

LUCY: Kate is going to take a shower…

IRENIE: Good idea.

LUCY: What are you looking at?

MAY: We've seen it. Their last show. At the Joyce.

IRENIE: It's going to be playing on the wall of your Mom's exhibit.

LUCY: I know. Suzanne told me.

SALLY: *(About the video)* The rest of us, we've pushed back against the back wall. See us in the shadows? As Rose does this crazy solo. I don't think she rehearsed this… *(Then. To* IRENIE:*)* We were all in tears. *(Then)* It wasn't planned, Lucy. Our walking off and leaving Rose alone. We just did it. To force her to take the last bow by herself…

DAVID: She was furious with you, I remember.

SALLY: She yelled at us later. 'We're a company!' She loved it…

(As she watches, we hear cheers and applause.)

*(*SUZANNE *will get up and bring a baking sheet of cut cauliflower to the stove. she will put it in the oven. And set a timer. and then wash her hands in the sink as:)*

SALLY: *(The video)* People giving her flowers. Everyone standing.

(On the phone: more cheers and applause)

SALLY: She doesn't take them. She is refusing… Unbelievable. She hated all that crap, Lucy.

LUCY: *(Smiles to* MAY*)* All that 'ballet stuff.'

SALLY: People are 'cautiously' setting flowers onto the lip of the stage… At least she's not throwing them back like she sometimes did…

(They laugh.)

SALLY: That's Maguy Marin…. *(To* LUCY*)* I forgot she was there.

SUZANNE: *(To* DAVID*)* She's going to be at the opening of the exhibit. She wrote a quote for the little booklet. Wrote nice things.

*(*SALLY *pauses the video.)*

SALLY: David? Remember the man—our closing night, coming up to the Joyce stage with the single rose?

IRENIE: We called him 'The mystery man'?

DAVID: I think so. Maybe. Why?

SALLY: He walked up with a single rose—for Rose. None of us could see his face.

IRENIE: *(To* LUCY*)* Alice's goddamn lights were right in our eyes.

SALLY: Now watch…

*(*SALLY *hands* DAVID *the phone. He starts the video and watches.)*

SALLY: There he is with his rose, and look, he *hands* her that single flower… And she *doesn't* throw it back… Why not? Why him?

IRENIE: That's why he was the mystery man, David.

(They watch.)

IRENIE: She bends down, takes it. And here she even does a bow to him, one of those goddamn stupid bows that every five year-old learns in ballet class, and that if we ever did one of those she'd scream at us…

SALLY: You are about to see who the mystery man was… You can him see on this. Freeze it…

*(*DAVID *does.)*

*(*DAVID *looks closely.)*

SALLY: *(To* LUCY*)* You know this?

SUZANNE: I told her.

SALLY: *(To* DAVID*)* See…?

DAVID: Fuck.

IRENIE: That's right.

DAVID: Fuck… Merce.

SALLY: It's Merce. Of course she'd bow to him… Probably the only guy on earth she would bow to.

IRENIE: She's bowing to Merce. That's him. Hat on. Long coat. The unmistakable face of Merce Cunningham.

DAVID: Suzanne, how in the world did you collect all this?

SUZANNE: My brother did a lot of it. Not just me.

LUCY: *(To* SUZANNE*)* You did most of the work.

SUZANNE: I know. I know. Did you eat on the train? I didn't ask if you'd eaten.

SALLY: *(Over this)* The line was too long.

LUCY: We had quiche for lunch… You want me to—?

IRENIE: We're good.

SALLY: You have any more of that cheese we had last night?

SUZANNE: I'll get it, Lucy. You should have said something. Of course you're hungry. Dinner's not for a while… *(She will start to go off.)*

SALLY: *(To* DAVID*)* There's going to be lots of photos too in the exhibit. Here…I took pictures of them.

(As DAVID *takes the phone and looks at the photos:)*

IRENIE: Suzanne has offered to scan the guest book, and send it to us.

SUZANNE: I think there will be a good crowd. It's been off and on, two, three times. It's a whole series the C N Ds are doing, dancers who died of Covid. *(She goes.)*

LUCY: One of A T D K's dancers wrote a very sweet note for the booklet.

SALLY: And Swinston. All sorts of people I wouldn't have expected. It's like a memorial. I'm glad we'll be there for the opening.

IRENIE: *(To* MAY*)* How's it going?

MAY: *(As she works)* Good.

DAVID: *(Looking at the photos)* Lucy, May, this, last engagement... We did six performances. Rose thought even that was too many. *(A voice)* 'I don't want to go out with empty seats.' Then when every damn seat sold, she's yelling at me 'we could have done ten, David!' So—my fault...

SALLY: It was your fault.

*(*SUZANNE *returns with the cheeses. She will get out plates, and napkins...)*

IRENIE: Suzanne...

SUZANNE: What?

IRENIE: Sally and I were just talking on the train about Merce and the last time we all were together.... You, your brother... You know what I'm talking about?

SUZANNE: No. I don't think so. There's May's bread.

SALLY: The butter?

SUZANNE: *(To* IRENIE*)* So when was this?

IRENIE: *Their* last show, Suzanne. At the Armory.

DAVID: Whose?

IRENIE: Merce's company. When they were disbanding after he died...

DAVID: I remember that, sure.

SUZANNE: Was that the last time we were together?

IRENIE: You and your brother made a special trip...

SUZANNE: Right. It was Christmas. *(To* LUCY*)* You know what we're talking about?

LUCY: I know.

SUZANNE: May doesn't know.

MAY: What?

SUZANNE: You'd have been about ten. Merce's company's last show, after he died.

MAY: I would have gone.

LUCY: I made Mom take me.

SUZANNE: I don't remember you being there.

DAVID: *(To* IRENIE*)* Tell May.

IRENIE: *(Continues)* There were three huge platforms set up in the Armory. You wandered around. They just danced. You chose what to watch. They weren't showing you anything. It's was like they were doing it all for themselves and we were flies on the wall. And everywhere you looked was amazing, May. I kept thinking, 'what am I missing over there?' And 'over there…'

SUZANNE: It was like that.

IRENIE: When it's over, no one wants to leave. They have to push us out onto the street.

DAVID: True.

IRENIE: Hundreds of people just standing out on Park Avenue. Not wanting to go home. And…Suzanne, did you ever hear this?

SUZANNE: I don't know what you're going to say.

DAVID: *(To* SALLY*, before she can ask)* I don't know.

IRENIE: We're out on the sidewalk and Rose and I overhear this young couple. A girl explaining to her boyfriend what she's now feeling. Now that it's all over. Rose loved telling this.

DAVID: *(To* SALLY*)* We have heard this.

IRENIE: I'm standing next to Rose and we hear this young woman say to her boyfriend: 'Imagine your favorite sports team suddenly is no more...' Then the girl corrects herself, 'No, no,—imagine that your favorite *sport* is no more. That's what I'm feeling now... That's what's been lost.'

DAVID: Before things shut down, Merce's dances were everywhere.

SALLY: It would have been his hundredth birthday...

*(*KATE *appears in the door; she has changed her clothes and has a bag with her.)*

LUCY: Kate...

IRENIE: *(Same time)* You all right, Kate?

DAVID: *(Same time)* There she is. She walks. Still standing. Good for you.

LUCY: There's cheese and bread...

KATE: I'm fine, Lucy. I'm not hungry.

DAVID: *(A joke)* She talks.

KATE: *(Over this)* I took a shower.

IRENIE: Sit down.

SALLY: *(About the bag)* What is that?

IRENIE: Sit down. Sit.

KATE: *(To* SALLY*)* I had it in my suitcase.

SALLY: You want more water? Hydrate...

KATE: I left my glass...

LUCY: You can use another glass. We have glasses...

MAY: I'll get it... *(She will get* KATE *water.)*

DAVID: Feel better?

KATE: *(Nods and as she sits)* So Rose stayed here...

SALLY: *(To* KATE*)* The apartment?

DAVID: Many many times. Suzanne and her brother had these dance conferences over the years. Rose and Alice always came.

KATE: I think you told me about them.

DAVID: I did.

SUZANNE: I usually put Rose and Alice up where the girls are. Your bedroom was my brother's. There still are some of his clothes…

KATE: On the dresser, there's a picture of you, Lucy, with your Mom. You're both smiling. You have braces…

LUCY: I couldn't wait to get them off.

KATE: *(Smiling)* I'm sure… And there's a photo of Rose with your brother, Jacques-Francois?

SUZANNE: That's him, yes.

SALLY: The first man in Rose's company.

IRENIE: *(Old joke:)* So we got to do lifts.

SUZANNE: He's lifting Rose in the photo…

(Lights fade.)

3.
Lucy.

(The same, a short time later)

*(*LUCY, MAY, SUZANNE *work on the dinner. Though now their focus is on* KATE.*)*

*(*KATE *is taking out a file from her bag.* IRENIE *is looking at a guidebook.)*

DAVID: Lucy, you sure you want to do this now?

SUZANNE: She told me she does.

KATE: Should we go into the living room…?

LUCY: I don't want to make this a big deal.

SUZANNE: Then it's fine. Give yourselves some room… Just move things…

(As the others clear a space:)

IRENIE: Suzanne, in Kate's guidebook it says Angers once called itself the 'Athens of the West.' Do people still call it that?

SUZANNE: Not with a straight face…. What does she have to sign?

KATE: Warren got them to me just before I left.

DAVID: *(Over this, to* SUZANNE*)* The lawyer in Rhinebeck.

KATE: Warren remembers you, Lucy. He sends his regards.

LUCY: *(To* DAVID*)* So you've sold Mom's house.

SALLY: We're selling it.

LUCY: Then it's not sold.

DAVID: There's a buyer. It happened like that. *(Snaps his fingers)*

SALLY: We should have asked for more…

DAVID: We keep asking ourselves that…

SALLY: *(To* LUCY*)* The boxes of stuff in the basement…?

DAVID: We rented a storage unit just outside the village on 9-G, by the pizza place.

LUCY: I know where you mean.

DAVID: We'll pay for that.

LUCY: Why?

DAVID: We want to.

SALLY: Kate's helping too.

DAVID: You can figure out what you want to do with all that stuff when you eventually come back. The rent's month to month. You'll need to give it more than a couple of days, there's a lot of stuff. As you know, everything goes to you. And unless you plan to be back in the next month—.

LUCY: I don't know that, Dad. I've told you that.

DAVID: I know you don't. And you have. And we understand.

SALLY: We've assumed that, Lucy.

DAVID: So then this... *(The paper)* is so I can sign for you at the closing of your mother's—your—house.

IRENIE: When is the closing?

SALLY: Two weeks, Irenie.

DAVID: Kate's renounced any claim, of course. You know that.

LUCY: I know that. Thank you, Kate.

KATE: I have a pension. An IRA. And I live very cheaply.

LUCY: You've been really good to Mom.

KATE: I loved her.

LUCY: I know. And she loved you, Kate.

DAVID: Lucy, do you know that there's not that much else besides the house?

SALLY: We've been worried that you think there's more than there now is... *(Then)* Do you know that your mom borrowed on the house?

LUCY: We didn't talk about money.

DAVID: I know that.

SALLY: *(Continues)* She had no pension. Just the social security. *(Shrugs)* She had a dance company...

DAVID: The social security has stopped, of course. *(To* SUZANNE*)* Months ago... When she died.

KATE: And she couldn't really live on that. Not with the taxes in Rhinebeck.

SALLY: And are there taxes.

LUCY: I know, Sally.

SALLY: Just when she got sick, the town did a new assessment. We both got burned. I don't know why. *(To* IRENIE*)* We got screwed. We should have fought it.

DAVID: Kate basically supported your mother for—well over a year. Throughout all the...the mess. Especially once she moved in with Kate... *(Then)* There's a credit card debt. She'd been paying off just the interest...

IRENIE: *(To* SALLY*)* You didn't tell me that.

SALLY: I forgot. *(To* LUCY*)* We talked about some of this on the train.

DAVID: So that has just been money down a hole. That was silly. She hadn't talked to me...

KATE: Me neither, Lucy. Then when I started paying her bills, I realized all this.

DAVID: *(To* LUCY*)* So it really is only the house. And then only after we pay off what she owed. So it's probably not what you expected. That's what Sal was saying. Maybe seventy, sixty-five thousand. Total. Maybe even a little less once everything...

SALLY: I think less.

DAVID: Maybe. But that's it.

SALLY: That may sound like a lot to you. But it's not.

IRENIE: No. It's not a lot today.

DAVID: The taxes alone...

LUCY: Let's do it, Dad.

SALLY: David, do you have your pen?

DAVID: I don't…

SUZANNE: I have one.

(SUZANNE gets up to get a pen. Hands it to LUCY as:)

SUZANNE: Lucy, you all right?

LUCY: I think so.

DAVID: You grew up in that house, I know.

SALLY: *(To LUCY)* There's furniture. We need to talk about how you want us to deal with that.

DAVID: And one more thing, that we wanted to tell you in person. You've been gone a long time. We're selling our house.

LUCY: Why?

DAVID: I know. Lucy. You grew up in that house too. But for the last year and a half your mom's house has been empty.

MAY: I stayed there.

SALLY: He meant she wasn't there. Rose.

DAVID: You did, May. And that was really nice… A big help. *(Then)* But Rose wasn't there. And we'd bought our house to be next to you and your mom, Lucy. That's pretty much the reason why we've been in Rhinebeck all these years. And now that reason is… The couple buying your mom's, they offered to buy ours. We hadn't really thought much about selling. Had we?

SALLY: A little bit.

DAVID: Mostly talk. Who doesn't talk about selling their house? And then they made a very good offer. *(Incredible)* A young couple. Your age, Lucy. He says he now can work from home…

SUZANNE: Why do they want two houses?

SALLY: Because they can? *(Shrugs)*

DAVID: The agent said, something to do with zoning; so they can build pretty much what the hell they want. I don't know… Tear down what they want. Without questions. Without neighbors.

SALLY: Suzanne, we'd taken over Lucy's college debts from her and Rose. So getting this money now for us is a kind of godsend.

SUZANNE: Right. Of course.

SALLY: And David's made nothing… Obviously, there have been no tours. There's been no theater. And even worse, he'd guaranteed two of his tours.

DAVID: I'm usually smarter than that.

SALLY: *(To* SUZANNE*)* So we're paying that back too. He has been getting unemployment…

DAVID: *(To* SUZANNE*)* First time I've gotten that. They changed the rules so someone like me could get that. It's helped. But…

KATE: When you come up to clean out the storage unit, you can stay with me. You know that. And of course you're always welcome…

(Then)

DAVID: I heard these kids talking about putting in a pool.

LUCY: There's a fucking lake!!

(This stops everyone.)

DAVID: The lake, they have to share, Lucy.

LUCY: I don't want to sell to them, Dad.

SALLY: The deal is done…

LUCY: It's my house.

DAVID: You told me to get what we can for it. So, we did…

(Short pause)

SUZANNE: So Sally, where are you going to live?

SALLY: We don't know yet… We're not sure.

DAVID: *(To* LUCY*)* I hear you, sweetie. But you don't really have a choice. You can't pay off her debts. You can't pay the taxes. You are not going to live in Rhinebeck.

LUCY: I don't know my plans. I don't know.

DAVID: And that too…

*(*LUCY *signs the paper.)*

(No one know what to say.)

SUZANNE: Dinner won't be ready for a while.

KATE: Let me show you some things. In this bag… *(She goes to the other bag she brought in.)* Maybe this is a good time?

IRENIE: For what?

KATE: I think it is.

LUCY: What, Kate?

KATE: *(As she gets the bag)* One day, when Rose still could, we spent an afternoon in her house. May, you weren't around. She had this idea… Lucy, this is for you.

(Then handing LUCY *a small box:)*

KATE: Here… This is from your mom. This has your name on it. Look.

IRENIE: *(To* SALLY*)* A present? From Rose?

(They all watch LUCY *take the box,* LUCY *looks at what is written.)*

KATE: Open it. *(To the others)* 'For Lucy.' And that is your Mother's handwriting, isn't it?

LUCY: Yes.

KATE: And believe me it got very hard for her to write anything. I said I would do it —. 'No!' Rose... *(Smiles)*

IRENIE: Open it.

(LUCY opens the box.)

LUCY: A bracelet... *(She holds it up.)*

SUZANNE: May I see?

SALLY: *(Leaning over)* Oh my God!

IRENIE: What?

SALLY: We all got one of these, remember?

IRENIE: Let me see, Lucy *(Smiling)* Yes! *(Laughs)* I still have mine.

SUZANNE: *(Over this)* I know I have mine.

SALLY: Read what it says on it... Read.

MAY: What does it say?

IRENIE: *(To MAY)* She made those up for her fiftieth birthday.

DAVID: *(To MAY)* She always organized her own birthdays. No one else could do it well enough...

MAY: What does it say?

LUCY: *(Reads)* "Tuck in your pelvis."

(Timer goes off.)

(SUZANNE will go to the oven and take out the tray of cauliflower and take it back to her work space.)

SUZANNE: I'll show you mine later. She once told me she'll go to her grave still reminding us of that.

LUCY: And now she has...

SUZANNE: Yeh.

IRENIE: *(To* LUCY*)* She gave them only to her dancers.

SALLY: Put it on…

IRENIE: *(Over this)* I'll bet that's the one she kept for herself, Lucy…

DAVID: You think that was hers? So that was your mother's. Neat.

IRENIE: *(Same time)* Let's see. Show us…

(As LUCY *puts on the braclet,* KATE *is taking an envelope out of the bag:)*

KATE: There's more. Suzanne… *(Reads)* "For Jacques Francois and Suzanne."

SUZANNE: Did she know he got married?

DAVID: We're staying with him. We can take it to him.

SUZANNE: Whatever it is, it stays here. Fuck him. *(Laughs. 'Explains')* Lucy invited him to dinner. His wife didn't want to come.

KATE: She was so thankful, Suzanne, that you and your brother were taking such good care of Lucy…

*(*SUZANNE *goes to get the gift.)*

SUZANNE: What is this?

KATE: Read what it says.

SUZANNE: "A nail from the outdoor deck at Jacob's Pillow."

(As SUZANNE *takes out a nail from the envelope, they laugh:)*

IRENIE: How the hell did she get that? I can just see her wandering around Jacob's Pillow in the dark with pliers… Oh Rose.

SUZANNE: I can make it into a necklace.

IRENIE: That could work.

*(*IRENIE *hands it to* SALLY.*)*

IRENIE: *(To* LUCY*)* Let me see the bracelet…

*(*LUCY *shows* IRENIE *as:)*

SALLY: *(To* SUZANNE*)* She was so upset about the fire last year….

IRENIE: *(About the fire)* Oh my god…

KATE: And here— 'May'…

MAY: For me? Why me?

*(*KATE *takes out a wrapped package.)*

KATE: *(Smiling)* Why? Because you were the biggest help… You were our godsend.

LUCY: What is it?

SALLY: It's wrapped. Come on, open it…

KATE: See? The word 'May' is pinned on it. That's my handwriting. She dictated that to me. Unwrap it. It's yours… From Aunt Rose.

(As MAY *unwraps it:)*

KATE: *(To* IRENIE *about* MAY*)* She did our shopping. She cleaned. She did a million things. A godsend.

SUZANNE: What is that? A dress…?

LUCY: It's a dress. Hold it up.

*(*MAY *holds it up.)*

IRENIE: Oh my god, I think I remember that dress.

SALLY: *(Over the end of this)* Me too! Me too. *That* dress.

SUZANNE: *(Over this)* Don't sell that, May. I know that dress.

MAY: *(Over this)* I won't. I won't. Why would I sell it?

LUCY: *(Over this)* Hold it up again.

KATE: *(To* LUCY*)* You know the dress?

*(*MAY *shows* LUCY *the dress.)*

DAVID: Let me see.

SUZANNE: That going to fit? That's not going to fit May.

KATE: It was in a suitcase….

MAY: I can't take this… How about you?

SUZANNE: *(To* LUCY*)* Your mother wore that dress.

LUCY: I know. It's for May, not me.

MAY: *(To* LUCY*)* I remember your mom in one of the videos in this dress…

LUCY: I know. I know.

IRENIE: *(To* SUZANNE*)* You're right, it's not going to fit you, May…

MAY: I don't think so.

LUCY: *(To* MAY*)* Try it on.

SALLY: It's not going to fit. What about Lucy?

KATE: No, Lucy doesn't want it.

LUCY: What are you talking about? Why do you say that?

KATE: This dress, you said you didn't want it.

LUCY: What are you talking about, Kate?

KATE: I asked your mom the same thing when I found that in the suitcase. I said, 'Rose, is this a costume?' And she said it was, and I said I'll bet Lucy would love to have this. And she said she'd offered it to you and you didn't want it.

SALLY: Is that true?

DAVID: Do you remember that?

KATE: So instead of putting it in the Salvation Army pile, Rose had me write 'May'.

LUCY: When I was like seventeen, Kate.

DAVID: What?

IRENIE: Oh my god.

LUCY: I said that when I was like seventeen. She wanted me to wear her dresses. And I didn't want to. When I was seventeen!

(DAVID *cringes.)*

SALLY: *(To* DAVID*)* It's not funny.

DAVID: I know. I'm not laughing. *(Explains everything)* Rose…

KATE: I guess that's just what she remembered, Lucy. She could get things mixed up…

SUZANNE: *(To* MAY*)* Give it to her. Lucy's more Rose's size, than May.

MAY: *(To* LUCY*)* You are.

(MAY *tries to hand it to* LUCY.*)*

DAVID: I think it would fit Lucy perfectly.

LUCY: She didn't give it to me, Dad.

DAVID: She tried. You and your mom were the same size.

LUCY: No, we weren't.

IRENIE: *(Over this)* It's too big for May. Look.

MAY: Try it on. It's not going to fit me, so what am I going to do with it? Come on, try it on…

SALLY: Put it on, Lucy. Why not?

IRENIE: Go ahead…

LUCY: *(To* MAY*)* It's yours. She gave it to you.

MAY: Not if it doesn't fit me… *(She heads off with the dress.)* It was your mom's…

(MAY *and* LUCY *are gone.)*

SUZANNE: Just try it on! Help her, May… *(Then)* Why not? *(Then)* She'll try it on…

(Off, church bells from the nearby church.)

IRENIE: Sally, when she was seventeen…

KATE: I'm sorry, I didn't know about the dress…

DAVID: Kate, it's not your fault. Rose…

(Lights fade.)

4.
I Don't Know.

(The same, a short time later.)

*(*SUZANNE *continues to work on the lasagna.)*

*(*DAVID *has gone back to working on the antipasto.)*

SUZANNE: It must have been really hard on you, Kate…

KATE: It was… At first she wouldn't accept things. *(Begins a list:)* That friends couldn't come in. Then we couldn't go out… Not even in the backyard. It had gotten cold. Her voice became soft. Very un-Rose. Really hard to hear. *(more of the list:)* 'Why can't Lucy come home?' 'Lucy can't come home. And even if she could, Rose—she can't come in here…' She was angry. 'I'm dying,' she said. 'I know, Rose. We all know…' And yet so full of energy and…

SUZANNE: And what?

DAVID: Rage.

*(*KATE *nods.)*

SUZANNE: That doesn't surprise me.

KATE: Which came right at me. Most of the time.

SUZANNE: I'm sorry.

KATE: It was the two of us. Just us. Almost all the time. May was great. She had Rose's car to drive. To get to Tops and anywhere else we needed her to go. And the two of us, Rose and me, we also had wonderful evenings together, Suzanne.

SUZANNE: She didn't see anyone—?

KATE: Not a soul. And I mostly talked with no one too. So she wouldn't feel bad. Wouldn't hear me on the phone. This woman who had spent a life in the center of…

DAVID: The party.

KATE: I was going to say 'of attention'. But that too. Did I answer your question, Suzanne?

SUZANNE: It wasn't really a question, Kate. *(Turns to* IRENIE:*)* And now you, Irenie…?

IRENIE: What has it been like for me? I spent a lot of time with my dog. They know that.

SALLY: Didn't she send you pictures?

SUZANNE: She sent me pictures.

IRENIE: Me and my dog.

SUZANNE: At least you didn't dress her up—

DAVID: Him.

SUZANNE: —up in costumes like half the world did with their dogs and cats. Thank god, you didn't do that.

(No response)

SUZANNE: Did she? It's okay.

IRENIE: *(Continues:)* Gibney's coming back. Very slowly. I wish them luck. I haven't gone back. I don't know why. I have a friend who said to me, and this seems so on the mark, she said, "everyone is now rethinking everything…" *(Then)* I was just waiting until I could come to Europe. That became the goal. Masked or unmasked. Even wrapped like a goddamn mummy, I didn't care. I told myself—just getting off the fucking plane will be some sort of—I don't know. I think I imagined it'd be like walking through a curtain into some neat, really busy room, with people laughing, piano music.

DAVID: Was it like that? When you got here?

IRENIE: Not yet.

(Smiles)

SALLY: My first trip back into the city, I thought it would feel strange. What surprised me is that it felt normal. And suddenly everything that'd come before—all of it—felt like a dream.

IRENIE: Does it still feel like that? With this variant?

SALLY: I guess not. Maybe not…

SUZANNE: What do you say we open the wine? I've had enough cider…David…?

*(*DAVID *gets up.)*

DAVID: Good idea.

IRENIE: *(Same)* I wouldn't say no.

SALLY: *(Over this)* I'm ready for wine…

SUZANNE: *(Over this)* On the floor next to the refrigerator…

IRENIE: *(To* SUZANNE*)* Can't I help with…?

SUZANNE: All under control, Irenie. Sit down. Relax.

*(*DAVID *starts to go off to get the wine.)*

SALLY: *(To* KATE*)* You. You should just stay with the water…

KATE: I can have wine.

DAVID: Any bottle?

SUZANNE: Any one…

(DAVID *goes off.)*

IRENIE: *(Continuing:)* I surprised myself, how happy I was to see a familiar face *(*SALLY*)* today. And meeting up with you too, Kate… So what else? To catch you up with…? I read *War and Peace.*

SALLY: So did I! *(Laughs)* David bought it for us.

IRENIE: I read some of it out loud to my dog. There's one little bit, *(To* SALLY*)* remember this?

SALLY: It's twelve hundred pages long.

IRENIE: I wrote this out and put it on my door so I'd see it when I went to take the garbage out, or the one day a week to the grocery store…

(DAVID *returns with a bottle of wine.)*

Pierre, he's a big character, he says this after having been through hell. He says: "As long as there's life, there's happiness. There's much, much still to come."

DAVID: *(Confused)* What?

SALLY: *War and Peace,* David. He gave up after fifty pages.

IRENIE: When you're alone you try and grab ahold of things. I watched so many of my friends let go…

SUZANNE: Here too.

IRENIE: *(Shrugs)* I don't know… *(Smiles)* I find I'm saying that to myself now ten times a day…

SALLY: What?

IRENIE: 'I don't know.' *(To* SUZANNE*)* Ask someone else now…

(SUZANNE *looks at* DAVID *who is opening wine and will get glasses and pour as:)*

DAVID: We talked last night.

SUZANNE: You talked to Lucy…

DAVID: Okay. Let's see. I don't know if this will even make sense for Sally and me. I have an offer.

IRENIE: Do I know about this?

SALLY: No.

DAVID: I haven't said yes. We're 'thinking' about it.

IRENIE: What kind of offer?

SALLY: A theater. Nick's a friend, someone David has been working with for years, and he's just been hired to run this theater. He wants David to join him. Do it together.

(DAVID *smiles.)*

Don't smile. It's not funny.

DAVID: It's not really a theater, it's a 'performing arts venue'. They mostly do rock concerts for kids.

SALLY: And they want to change that. That's why they wanted him. And you.

IRENIE: Where is this theater?

SALLY: Utica. May's mom knows the theater.

IRENIE: Utica? Rose always made a joke of Utica.

DAVID: She'd find this so funny, Kate.

SALLY: It's an interesting sort of place.

DAVID: You haven't been.

SALLY: *(Ignoring him)* I've read about it. Utica has attracted a lot of refugees from wars all around the world. Bosnia. Vietnam…

IRENIE: Afghanistan?

SALLY: I'm sure. If not now, soon enough. It's an inexpensive place to live. Irenie, I was thinking maybe I can teach kids there dance.

IRENIE: They probably don't have a lot of modern dance teachers…

DAVID: I'm guessing that's true.

SALLY: And we can't do nothing, David. I can't. The longer one sits in a chair the harder it is to get up.

DAVID: *(Smiles)* You hear that on N P R?

SALLY: *(Smiles)* I did. Anyway, we're not going to live our lives depressed.

DAVID: I'm not depressed. I haven't been depressed. Why do you say that?

SALLY: Anyway, 'we don't know'. Like you, Irenie. 'We don't know'… Not yet. David took his social security earlier than he'd wanted to.

IRENIE: *(To* DAVID*)* I have friends who had to do that too. Actors…

DAVID: I've missed my life, Suzanne. One day it dawned on me, I hadn't gone this long without seeing a play or a dance since I was—and this is absolutely true—like ten years old. *(Then)* I kept on thinking: what I wouldn't give to be sitting in a theater right now…

SUZANNE: Kate… We're back to you.

KATE: You skipped Sally…

SALLY: That was just me too. Me and David. Your turn.

KATE: What more should I tell?

SALLY: *(Starting a list:)* Getting married…

KATE: *(To* SUZANNE, *her list)* Rose and I got married.

SUZANNE: I know that.

KATE: *(To* SALLY*)* So what's to tell?

SUZANNE: *(To* KATE*)* Rose refused to do the wedding on Zoom. Why was that? Lucy was hurt you didn't. Felt cut out…

KATE: It's not how Rose wanted it. I don't know why. She wouldn't say why. I think it's not how she wanted her daughter to see her.

SALLY: Suzanne, David and I stood outside in coats and masks. Watched through Kate's dining room window. A wedding in the middle of a pandemic.

KATE: Rose once said to me, Suzanne: "The moment I gave birth to her, it was like my heart began walking around outside of me." She did miss Lucy. I've never had children. *(Then. More list:)* I've got her ashes in my kitchen. They've been there for nearly six months. They're waiting for something...

DAVID: When Lucy comes back, Kate.

KATE: When is that?

*(*MAY *enters.)*

SUZANNE: What do you need?

MAY: A seam's ripped in the dress...

SUZANNE: The sewing basket's in the closet.

MAY: I just looked—.

SUZANNE: On the top shelf, May...I saw it there this morning... Look harder. Top shelf. Look...

*(*MAY *goes.)*

KATE: Suzanne... Now your turn...

SUZANNE: I should get this in....*(The lasagna)* If we ever want to eat... *(She will put the lasagna in the oven:)*

KATE: You just can't ask questions. What happened to you? I know your brother got married. And that was hard. *(Then)* You'd been living together...?

SUZANNE: For twenty-six years...

(Then)

IRENIE: Suzanne...

SUZANNE: What do you want me to say? *(As she sets the timer.)* I asked him—what happened? He said, 'I got scared.' 'Of what?' I said. He didn't know. He said, 'All we have, are our relationships. Being alone is a tragedy.'

IRENIE: He said that, and then he left you alone?

SUZANNE: Yeh. He said, he got scared and so that's what he did. He got married.

IRENIE: He was always so fucking spoiled.

SUZANNE: Lucy was here for all of this.

DAVID: I know.

SUZANNE: I'm sorry she was, having to see me like that. She's a strong young woman. She was a help. I wasn't very nice. I wasn't happy.

DAVID: She's seen a lot.

SUZANNE: Has she. She and I danced together in here. A lot.

IRENIE: In the kitchen?

SUZANNE: We had a dance party with our shadows! Her idea. And she knows French now.

KATE: That's incredible.

SUZANNE: *(Not incredible)* She's been here a year and a half, Kate. *(Then)* It all just went on and on.

IRENIE: Yeh.

SUZANNE: That is the feeling. Of it never going to come to an end. At first when it was a few months: 'Oh my God, why are we closing the theaters? We're working! We are essential workers too! We're dancers!'

IRENIE: I don't think American dancers argued that.

SUZANNE: And then—I don't think you had this—it made it worse. We went back to work as if nothing had happened. 'It's all over.' 'In the past.' A few wore masks, but not that many did. We hugged. Went to bars. And again the door closed. And again. And again. You felt like some sort of animal hiding away in your goddamn little hole. Where is everybody? What are other people doing? I tried to teach a dance class on Zoom? Try that sometime.

DAVID: Sally has.

SALLY: My god…

SUZANNE: Might as well just punch yourself in the face, it's the same sort of reward… *(Then)* And again we have to lock ourselves in. Dance in the kitchen… What to believe? Begins to feel like a wound that won't heal, hurts when you touch it or bump it against something. Then it hurts like hell. It was supposed to be almost normal now. If you're vaccinated. But it's not, is it? Not yet. So when? *(Then)* Having Lucy here through everything, and now May these past two months…I sometimes sit here alone and think what am I going to do when they are gone? *(Then)* There's a dance in tomorrow's festival. It's the finale. My brother made this dance. I don't think I'm spoiling it… You'll see it tomorrow. The dancers go out into the lobby—which is huge, like an airplane hanger. And they all start six feet apart, dancing their individual dances from their presentations. Then they get closer to each other. Five feet. Four feet. Three feet. Until all are dancing together, bumping off of each other, holding on to each other…

(Short pause)

DAVID: After a while Sally and I got very—

SALLY: What?

DAVID: Very good at bridge.

SALLY: *(A joke)* I thought he was going to say—we got very 'close'.

DAVID: We also tried Animal Crossing.

SUZANNE: Kate, tell me more about Rose… Lucy and I spent so much time talking about her…

KATE: *(Hesitates, then)* She'd planned over and over how she wanted to die. Really thought about it.

DAVID: *(To* SUZANNE*)* She did. In great detail.

KATE: How she wanted to say good bye. And then—she couldn't. It wasn't the cancer… but the virus now. That was the kick in the stomach. You're ready, you prepare yourself, for one thing and then… And then you can't even be together. You can't hold hands. Can't touch. Kiss. There was an awful pain just in that. *(Then)* We never once said the word 'goodbye'. We couldn't. Not through a nurse's borrowed fucking IPad… That's what she was left with. To hold onto. Nice people tried to help. But… Into an IPad… That is not how you imagine… "There's no goddamn dignity left." Rose said that… *(Stops. Then)* We didn't know how she caught it. We'd been really really careful; she was very ill and weak. Of course we were careful. It started with a fever; she didn't want to go to the hospital… She didn't want to get tested. She fought me. She wanted to be home. And so she got angry with me… But then she couldn't breathe. That scared me. I'd gotten my shots. She hadn't. Who the hell was going to come to the house to give her a fucking shot? *(She stops.)*

SUZANNE: What?

KATE: With Rose in the hospital, trying to breathe, for some perverse reason, some friend of May's, I think, suggested to May that May go and get a test for antibodies… And yes, she's positive. *(Then)* May comes in one day to my house, after Rose is gone, and she is very pale. She's upset. 'What's wrong, May?' And she says to me, she says—'Kate, was it me?' 'Did she get it from me?' 'Of course not,' I said. 'Don't be silly. Of course not.' So does this wonderful girl now live with that question?

(Then)

SALLY: Suzanne, has May ever mentioned this?

SUZANNE: No. Never.

KATE: Good. Then maybe she believed me… Maybe. But she is good at hiding her feelings…

SALLY: I know. She is.

(No one knows what to say, then:)

IRENIE: *(To* DAVID *and* SALLY*)* So—Utica.

DAVID: I don't know. I don't know, Irenie.

SALLY: Let's talk about it. His friend Nick offered David a job to come to Utica and work with him.

KATE: Why Utica?

SALLY: It's where this theater is, Kate. *(To* DAVID*)* And it's not just for rock concerts; it was built as a real theater. There's a balcony, the boxes are still there, haven't been torn off like in a lot of places. Eight hundred seats. *(Then)* Nick and David have worked together for years. Nick's just left his theater in the city. He thought he'd try and teach, but then this came along in Utica.

DAVID: I don't know…

SALLY: Let's talk to them, David. They're our friends. Let's talk.

DAVID: Nick visited us in Rhinebeck just before we left. Stayed the night. I asked him if he felt that this—Utica—was him running away?

IRENIE: From…?

DAVID: He said to me, after a few drinks, "David, I really don't think my theater's a 'white theater'. I have never seen it that way. Maybe I'm wrong… Am I wrong?" I didn't know what to say to that. I don't know.

SALLY: You listened.

DAVID: I did. *(Then)* "David,' he said, 'I don't think I'm a racist. But is that for me to say? Can I say that?" "It's such a crazy time…" he said. *(He looks to* SALLY. *Then)* There'd been a meeting with his whole staff a while ago. On Zoom of course. Everything's been on fucking Zoom. It was supposed to be about basic general stuff—Covid stuff. Where are they now? Who's getting furloughed, why, and maybe for how long? At this meeting some of his staff, they attack him.

SALLY: *(Correcting him)* Criticize him, David.

DAVID: Criticize him, you're right. He's completely unprepared for this. He's confused. Or is he clueless? He asked that too. No one stood up for him… There were plenty of people on that staff he'd mentored… *(Then)* He said he spent that night and the next and the next asking questions: What can I do? How can I help? Should I help? What have I done wrong? Have I done wrong? Is it just who I am? What I am? What can I say? To whom? When? And do I need to believe what I say, or can I just say what I think I am supposed to say?" "I don't know, David", he said. "I don't know." *(Then)* When he resigned from his theater, Irenie, he said he got a lot of phone calls—commiserating, praising him. People he'd worked with for years. But almost no emails. No letters. He said, 'almost nothing in writing…' Crazy time…I don't know.

(Then)

IRENIE: You've been up to Utica?

SALLY: No. Not yet. This just happened.

DAVID: I've been.

SALLY: Not for years, David. Nick showed us pictures. A local orchestra plays in there too, Irenie. And it seems to be a nice space even for dance...

SUZANNE: So you can bring in dance companies... So it's not been just for kids.

SALLY: I have my doubts too.

SUZANNE: Something new. An adventure. Turn the page.

DAVID: Maybe. I don't know. I don't know...

SALLY: I don't know either. *(She laughs.)*

(Then)

SUZANNE: Lucy's had a very good time here, I think, David.

DAVID: I know that.

SUZANNE: And May too, Kate...I think.

KATE: Good.

SUZANNE: So your money wasn't wasted, Kate.

KATE: I'm not worried about my money, Suzanne.

SUZANNE: I know that, Kate.

KATE: *(Over this)* Lucy wrote me that she's doing Rose's old dances? For her presentation. I was surprised. I was worried—can she do that?

SUZANNE: She's adapted them. Made them her own. So now they're her own. But I worry they might come across a bit old fashioned now. Decades old. From another time.

IRENIE: I'm a little worried about that too.

SUZANNE: Lucy doesn't care. She's—she's pretty stubborn. If you hadn't noticed.

DAVID: Oh really! *(Laughs)*

SUZANNE: Kate, the other day, she came home and said to me— 'Mom keeps giving me notes.' I laughed. What are you talking about? I asked what she meant. She said in the studio, when she's alone, her mom gives her notes. And—she tries not to hear her. And Lucy said, sometimes her mom's really hard on her… *(Then)* Lucy doesn't always tell you what she's feeling or thinking….

DAVID: What a surprise.

KATE: I know.

SUZANNE: So you have to get hints.

KATE: Like what?

SUZANNE: There's a girl here. Lucy's gotten to know her. From Romania. She's done this dance that Lucy watches whenever they rehearse. She makes a point of doing that. I don't how many times she's seen it.

KATE: What's the dance?

SUZANNE: Three girls cry. Just cry, Kate. But very theatrically. Gasp, heave, shake. At first it's upsetting. And just hysterical. Hard to watch. Then, and you don't really know how this happens, but imperceptibly, these three girls' bodies begin to be synchronized—and this awful crying, this misery, their pain has turned into dance.

KATE: And this is what she's watched a lot? Crying that becomes dance?

(SUZANNE *nods.)*

KATE: Rose would have understood that, I think.

DAVID: Suzanne, has she talked at all about what she wants to do?

SUZANNE: No. Not to me. Maybe May.

SALLY: We don't know anything.

KATE: No, we don't.

SUZANNE: Me too. She's still hurt. I know she feels the loss of her mom every day. You've already seen that... Jacques-Francois is great with her. I give him that. They get along really well. It's like they have their own language now. He got upset at one of the teachers here. He's an idiot. My brother hates him. They can really have a stick up their ass, the French.

IRENIE: You're French.

SUZANNE: At an assembly, he stood up in front of everyone—all the kids, and made a speech; 'There's no place here for people to start getting on stage and telling us about their horrible childhood, their terrible boyfriends, their parents, what it feels like to have your period. Keep it to yourself. Self-obsession has no place here... This isn't Twitter. This isn't America."

DAVID: He said that?

SUZANNE: He did. Lucy found it funny. I thought she'd be offended but... My brother said he was looking right at Lucy. *(Then)* Let me go and see what the girls are doing. They should be here with you... Kate just arrived. You came all this way... They should be in here...

KATE: I'm fine.

*(*SUZANNE *goes off.)*

KATE: It sounds like it hasn't been that easy for Lucy here...

SALLY: "This isn't America..." Fuck him.

IRENIE: And so Jacques-Francois has been a big help. He's been looking out for her.

SALLY: That doesn't surprise me.

IRENIE: Me neither.

DAVID: Sally, this morning at breakfast after you left for the train, Jacques-Francois said there have been moments when he's been working with Lucy on a dance—when he forgot himself and thought he was talking to Rose.

*(*MAY *and then* LUCY *enter.)*

*(*LUCY *now in her mom's dress.)*

*(*SUZANNE *is right behind them.)*

MAY: It fit Lucy.

DAVID: Oh wow. My god...

SALLY: I don't believe it.

LUCY: Feel it. I love the way it feels, Irenie.

IRENIE: And obviously moves.

LUCY: Look... Look at this... Touch it.

SALLY: It's a dance dress. It's made to move.

MAY: That's what I said.

IRENIE: *(To* KATE*)* Like Rose just walked in.

DAVID: That's what I'm thinking too.

MAY: Kate, I think it smells of Aunt Rose.

KATE: Maybe it's the moth balls...

LUCY: No, it smells of Mom. It really does...

SALLY: She wore that dress a lot. Danced in that a lot.

(They all look at LUCY.*)*

IRENIE: Perfect fit.

DAVID: They were the same size.

IRENIE: Turn round…I'd really love to see her dance in that dress.

MAY: I think she should wear that in her show.

SUZANNE: Why don't you see how it feels? Dance in it.

LUCY: Go to the studio, Suzanne?

SUZANNE: Why not in here? We dance in here all the time. And I'm sure they'd love to see.

IRENIE: Is Lucy going to dance?

LUCY: What should I do?

SUZANNE: What would go with that dress?

LUCY: I don't know….I don't know how I'd feel…

DAVID: Feel about what?

LUCY: It was Mom's.

(Lights fade.)

5.
The Dance Festival.

(The same, a short time later)

*(*SUZANNE *and* SALLY *are rolling up a rug.)*

MAY: *(With an IPhone)* I have it *(The song)*, Lucy…

LUCY: We've got it, Dad. Sit.

DAVID: I wanted to help.

MAY: David, stay there.

SUZANNE: *(Again:)* We dance in my kitchen all the time.

SALLY: Like home.

IRENIE: Are those chairs in the way?

SUZANNE: They are…

MAY: I've got this one.

KATE: You're going to dance?

LUCY: Suzanne taught it to me... You're fine here, Kate.

SUZANNE: *(To* IRENIE*)* You're good there.

LUCY: Mom danced this, Kate. This was her dance. Sit there, Dad...

SUZANNE: Sit... Sit... Sh-sh...

(The others settle.)

MAY: *(To* KATE*)* Watch...

LUCY: May...

MAY: And... *(She plays the music:)*

*(*Miss Otis Regrets *sung by Maxine Sullivan)*

MAY: Loud enough?

*(*LUCY *nods.)*

IRENIE: I remember this.

DAVID: I do too.

*(*LUCY *begins to dance. As the others watch, they remember Rose dancing this, and see an image of Rose in* LUCY, *in that dress. They share looks, smiles, get lost in thought as* LUCY *dances:)*

(And after a minute or so LUCY *stops dancing:* MAY *hands her the IPhone and she stops the music.)*

LUCY: Then my dancers come in, drag me around, lift me up. You'll see tomorrow.

IRENIE: The dress is perfect for that dance.

SALLY: I love it. Wear it.

DAVID: That was beautiful, Lucy. *(To* SALLY*)* So Rose.

SALLY: It was. It is.

SUZANNE: She dances it well, doesn't she?

(Others agree.)

SUZANNE: And I think that dress really works.

DAVID: Just like your Mom.

LUCY: I'm not Mom, Dad. Please don't say that.

DAVID: I didn't mean—. I meant….

LUCY: Do you think it's too long?

SUZANNE: How did it feel?

LUCY: Felt fine.

SUZANNE: Then wear it.

LUCY: I open my presentation with this dance, Kate.

KATE: And you danced that dance for Rose, Lucy.

LUCY: I wondered if you'd remember.

KATE: Of course I remember.

IRENIE: What do you mean?

LUCY: *(Over this)* Last winter. On Zoom.

SUZANNE: I followed her, holding her laptop.

DAVID: *(To* SALLY*)* I didn't know that.

SALLY: *(Same time)* I didn't know.

LUCY: *(Over this)* The last thing Mom ever saw me dance. And she liked it, right, Kate? Mom? Liked how I danced?

KATE: It was all she could talk about, for weeks…

LUCY: She didn't say much to me.

KATE: I wrote you and told you how much it meant to her.

LUCY: I know. I know that.

IRENIE: Only Rose ever dance that dance… She wouldn't let anyone else.

LUCY: I know. Suzanne learned it just to teach it to me…

SUZANNE: Lucy, the first time I ever saw Rose Michael, she was wearing that dress, in a dance.

SALLY: I think she wore it a lot.

DAVID: There weren't a lot of dresses. We had no money.

SUZANNE: *Blue Eyed Blues*. That was the dance. I danced that too, but without the dress.

IRENIE: May danced *Blue Eyed Blues,* Suzanne. In Rose's retrospective last year. You still remember it?

(As MAY *dances a few steps from* Blue Eyed Blues*:)*

SUZANNE: She's doing it in the fringe…

IRENIE: Look at her…

SALLY: Go girl…

IRENIE: Good for you.

MAY: *(As she stops dancing)* In the fringe we dance what the hell we want.

DAVID: Kate, the fringe around Lucy's festival…

SALLY: *(To* SUZANNE*)* That's tonight?

LUCY: Dad, wait until you see my dancers. There are so many really talented kids here…

SUZANNE: They're not all kids.

LUCY: *(An example)* Charlie…

DAVID: *(To* MAY*)* Who's—?

MAY: He's like twenty, twenty-one, David. He dances for Lucy. Does his own things too.

LUCY: Everyone wants him. He's got his own presentation. May's dancing in that too.

MAY: He's cool. Looks eighteen. He's American too.

LUCY: Charlie's been living in Brussels. Going to the dance school there.

IRENIE: *(Obviously)* De Keersmaker's.

LUCY: *(Over this)* He did this solo and I loved what he said about the response he got from one of his teachers. He was so happy.

SALLY: What response?

MAY: *(Over this)* He acts like a kid.

LUCY: Dad, his advisor had told him that his dance was—this was the word: 'childlike'. *That* made him happy. *(To* MAY*)* Didn't it? In Brussels his teachers kept saying his work was 'childish.'

MAY: So he was improving.

DAVID: That's funny.

MAY: *(Over this)* He's really great.

LUCY: Charlie says he's not going back to the States, Dad.

DAVID: What do his parents think about that?

LUCY: He doesn't care.

SALLY: Can we see everything? Or do we have to choose programs?

SUZANNE: Nothing's at the same time. So everything if you're up for it. Tell them about your friend Sarah. She only works with amateurs. This is neat.

LUCY: She's gotten together about forty local women…

IRENIE: That can't be easy.

SUZANNE: She has to work with them at night or weekends.

MAY: They all have jobs.

LUCY: She gets them in a long line.

SALLY: What ages…?

MAY: All ages, Sally.

SUZANNE: Up to age ninety… Different backgrounds, professions, cultures, races.

LUCY: They line up and she calls out a name—a famous woman's name.

DAVID: Like who?

LUCY: 'Beyonce.'

(They laugh.)

KATE: Beyonce?

LUCY: And the women and girls and little girls then walk toward the audience as if they all were 'Beyonce.'

*(*LUCY *and* MAY *mime a little 'Beyonce'.)*

IRENIE: That's fun.

SALLY: I like this dance.

KATE: What does it mean?

SUZANNE: Whatever they want it to, Kate.

DAVID: *(To* KATE*)* It just is itself.

LUCY: Then they hurry back, and another name is called out, say— 'Angela Merkel.'

*(*LUCY *and* MAY *do a little 'Angela Merkel' as:)*

MAY: She stoops a little forward…

IRENIE: Funny. We'll see this?

SUZANNE: The Australian girl, May… Her dance.

MAY: A minister comes to preach to a factory of women prisoners.

LUCY: When Australia was a penal colony. This really happened.

MAY: As he starts to preach, we women all pull up our skirts and begin, in unison, to slap our bare butts to drown him out. That's the dance. She's got everybody doing it.

SUZANNE: *(As she slaps her butt)* I'm doing it.

MAY: Jacques Francois wanted to do it too. We told him 'Only Women'!

(Laughter)

SUZANNE: Can I tell them what you call your presentation, Lucy? The title?

LUCY: I'll tell them— 'I Watched My Mother Dance with Her Friends.' What I remember. My memory.

DAVID: Of your Mom?

LUCY: Yeh, I guess.

SUZANNE: When she was a little kid, she watched us a lot, remember?

SALLY: Oh I remember…Rose always saying, 'don't step on the kid.'

SUZANNE: *(To* LUCY*)* Maybe you should take the dress off before anything happens to it.

LUCY: I'm careful. I can—.

SUZANNE: What?

LUCY: I can show them another of my dances… May, *South Ramparts?*

SALLY: *South Ramparts?* We all danced that.

IRENIE: We did. We danced that.

LUCY: *(Over this)* I know. I've changed a few things, Sal.

SUZANNE: You've changed a lot.

(As LUCY *gets ready:)*

LUCY: Six of us are in this.

SUZANNE: You going to wear the dress?

LUCY: I don't want to change, Suzanne.

MAY: From the top?

LUCY: Yeh. May's in this... Actually, it starts with May.

DAVID: Who needs to move?

LUCY: We're good, Dad. Just Kate needs to move...

KATE: What—?

DAVID: They're going to dance, Kate.

KATE: I know that.

LUCY: *(To* KATE*)* I think you'll be safer over there...

KATE: Safer?

IRENIE: I'm going to move too. Over here, Kate. Sit here... Best seat in the house.

KATE: Is it?

SUZANNE: *(Again:)* We dance in here all the time.

SALLY: Is Irenie good there? *(To* SUZANNE*)* Is she?

SUZANNE: You're fine.

LUCY: Ready, May? Settle down. Everyone settled? *(With the IPhone)* And...

(South Rampart Street *[Bob Crosby & His Orchestra—instrumental])*

MAY: Can it be louder...?

LUCY: I'll move this *(Speaker)* closer...

*(*LUCY *plays the start of the music.)*

LUCY: How's this...?

*(*MAY *nods.)*

*(*LUCY *starts the music again and* MAY *begins her solo.)*

(She dances.)

(The others laugh, remembering themselves dancing this; noticing changes that LUCY *has made to the dance.)*

LUCY: Do you recognize this, Irenie?

MAY: *(Dancing)* I love this…

*(*MAY *stops for a moment, and* LUCY *explains as the music continues:)*

LUCY: Here, Charlie enters. He does this with jumps. Amazing jumps.

SALLY: The American boy.

*(*MAY *and* LUCY *demonstrate a bit.)*

LUCY: Big jumps…

SUZANNE: He's very good. Charlie.

LUCY: Even more jumps. And then—Gwyneth's solo.

MAY: You want me to?

LUCY: No, I'll do it. Gwyneth's solo. I don't dance this.

(Music changes LUCY *dances.)*

MAY: Sally, and do you recognize this?

IRENIE: That's your part Sal… You never looked so tall…

(And LUCY *dances.)*

LUCY: *(Dancing)* It's fun in Mom's dress.

SALLY: Rose stole that from Paul Taylor.

IRENIE: She did.

LUCY: *(Dancing)* All four girls are dancing now…

SUZANNE: I was one of those girls.

SALLY: *(To* DAVID*)* What are you thinking?

DAVID: *(Obviously)* Like her mom.

SALLY: Me too. Me too.

(They go 'off' and return:)

LUCY: *(Dancing)* Now six—of us here… I'm now Mom.

*(*MAY *and* LUCY *exit and return dancing.)*

(And they finish the dance and 'exit' to applause and cheers.)

IRENIE: Take a bow.

SALLY & DAVID: Take a bow.

*(*MAY *and* LUCY *take a bow.)*

SUZANNE: Have some water…

LUCY: *(Out of breath)* You'll see it with all my dancers tomorrow. It's better with six, but you get the idea…

IRENIE: Jacques Francois always hammed up the jumps.

SALLY: He really did.

DAVID: Like your mother's but different…

LUCY: Not as good, Dad?

DAVID: I said 'different', Lucy…

LUCY: *(Out of breath)* We watched the video of you guys. Jacques Francois and Suzanne then started us off. And then we went from there…

DAVID: *(To* LUCY*)* That's why it's different. And that's the point. Isn't it? To have it be yours *and* your mom's…

(Timer goes off.)

*(*SUZANNE *gets up.)*

LUCY: Is that the point? I don't know. Is there a point?

SALLY: *(To* SUZANNE*)* Is it ready? I think here comes dinner.

SUZANNE: Are you starving? Have you been waiting—?

DAVID: *(Over the end of this)* We've been smelling it, Suzanne. We're sitting in the kitchen.

SUZANNE: I'm sorry if it's taken too long.

DAVID: Are we eating?

SUZANNE: Not yet. Not yet. It'll need to cool a little. Another ten, fifteen minutes. Can you wait that much longer? You have to wait. *(She takes the lasagna out of the oven.)*

LUCY: May, how about *My Dad Courts My Mom?*

DAVID: What?

SUZANNE: Catch your breath first.

LUCY: There's one called *My Dad Courts My Mom.*

IRENIE: A dance?

DAVID: *(To* SUZANNE*)* What is this?

SUZANNE: *My Dad Courts My Mom,* a dance, David. That's what your daughter calls it.

SALLY: I'd like to see this dance.

DAVID: I'm not sure I do. *(To* LUCY*)* So I'm a part of your show?

LUCY: Jacques Francois remembered Mom making this dance years ago. He said it never worked out, never got shown. Because one day Alice saw a run through and just hated it. Made Mom throw it out… *(Then)* I dance Dad. With May. Our duet. May, can you find the music…?

MAY: Start from the beginning?

*(*MAY *will find the music on the IPhone.)*

LUCY: *(Nods)* Kate, Mom was always saying that Dad grew up in hillbilly country. And that that explained everything.

DAVID: What did it explain? *(The thousandth time)* And I grew up in a city. In West Virginia. Your Mom visited there once for like two hours…

KATE: You're from West Virginia?

DAVID: What is wrong with that?

KATE: Nothing. Nothing.

IRENIE: Should we move?

SUZANNE: *(Pointing)* You're fine there. They dance around there.

LUCY: *(With the IPhone)* May, is it set? Play it loud…

(As LUCY *walks off to make an entrance:)*

SALLY: *My Dad Courts My Mom.* You worried?

DAVID: I don't know. Maybe…

MAY: Lucy, ready…? Everyone settled? And…

*(*SALLY *starts the music:* West Virginia Man *by David Allen Coe.)*

*(*LUCY *makes an entrance, dancing.)*

LUCY: A West Virginia Man…

(The others are soon laughing, drinking; wine is poured, they are relaxing. Having fun.)

(After LUCY *has danced for a while,* MAY *makes her 'entrance'.)*

IRENIE: Oh and I think here comes Rose. To be courted!

*(*LUCY *and* MAY *dance a duet:)*

KATE: *(Laughing)* Rose would have loved this.

(Others enjoy her laughing.)

(And as the song ends, MAY *as 'Rose' runs out of the run with* LUCY *as her 'dad' chasing her.)*

(Applause, cheers. The girls return.)

IRENIE & OTHERS: Bow!! Bow!

(The girls do a bow.)

SALLY: David, I like you in a dress.

DAVID: I didn't wear the pants.

LUCY: *(Out of breath)* So, Dad?

DAVID: What is so wrong with West Virginia?

SALLY: You've never looked so cute… Don't be so defensive.

LUCY: *(To* MAY*)* I got a little ahead or myself. Always the same place…

DAVID: Kate, and that is pretty much how Rose and I courted. Just for the record. Actually exactly like that. I flailed and she wriggled away.

LUCY: Kate, you okay?

KATE: I just wish Rose were here.

DAVID: She would have loved seeing this, Lucy.

IRENIE: *(A joke)* Her dress is here…

SUZANNE: The title for the whole festival is 'What You Can't Say, You Dance.'

DAVID: And, Lucy, what can't you say?

LUCY: *(Out of breath)* 'I love you, Mom.'

DAVID: Why can't you say that?

LUCY: *(Out of breath)* Because she's not here, Dad. Suzanne, when's dinner? How much longer?

SUZANNE: This has to cool. You going to do another one?

LUCY: *(To* MAY*, the title) "May's Mom's Cocktail Hour.'*

SUZANNE: That answers my question.

LUCY: *(Out of breath)* May… You explain.

MAY: This dance we have set in a motel in beautiful Utica, New York.

SALLY: Utica, David…

DAVID: I heard. You Mother's motel?

SUZANNE: We all danced this one too, with Rose.

SALLY: A dance about Rose's sister…? Hence the motel?

MAY: Yes, my dear mother, Sally.

LUCY: My aunt.

SALLY: Your sister-in-law, David

KATE: Mine too.

SALLY: That's right, she is.

MAY: In that motel where I grew up… And where pretty much every afternoon, precisely at the stroke of four-thirty, my mother and her very best friends gathered in the motel's living room with its fake wood paneling and smell of disinfectant, and where, unless I was lucky enough to hide or be sick, I had the job of serving them—cocktails…

SUZANNE: Jacques Francois showed them a tape of this, and May said… What did you say?

MAY: 'I want to do that. That's my Mom!'

(Laughter)

DAVID: May, I like your mother.

SALLY: Since when?

MAY: I do too. She's my mother.

SUZANNE: *(To* LUCY*)* Did you find the music?

(She had.)

LUCY: Sal, can you…? *(The music)*

IRENIE: So we all danced this one?

SUZANNE: All of us…Lucy's changed things. But you'll recognize it.

LUCY: As a kid, I remember sitting in the rehearsal room, curled up in the corner, eyes wide open, watching you all dance this. *(To* MAY*)* Let's stand as far back as we can.

IRENIE: I don't know which dance this is.

SUZANNE: You'll see…

LUCY: I think we're ready…

SALLY: Here goes… And…

(Music: Spike Jones' rendition of Cocktails for Two.*)*

*(*LUCY *and* MAY *start slowly to dance.)*

DAVID: Oh no. I know this.

KATE: What?

*(*IRENIE *and* SALLY *also recognize this.)*

SALLY: Nooo!

(Laughter)

DAVID: Just wait. Just wait.

IRENIE: I remember Rose teaching us this…

SALLY: Me too…

DAVID: *(To* KATE*)* Have you met Rose's sister?

KATE: No. Not yet. She wasn't allowed to visit.

DAVID: She's not a bad person… *(To* SALLY*)* Not all the time…

SUZANNE: May so wanted to dance this…

(And then as this version goes crazy with silly sound effects the dance becomes wild.)

(Whoopee, whistle, bang)

(Horn noises)

(Clink clink) …

(Wheezing cough)

(Etc)

IRENIE: I need this…

DAVID: *(A joke)* May should be ashamed of herself. She's her mother!

(They are laughing, enjoying themselves.)

SALLY: *(To* DAVID*)* Her mother is like that…

DAVID: I know. I know…

(A musical interlude with hiccups and other strange noises when:)

(They stop dancing before the song ends, laughing, the others are laughing; LUCY *takes the IPhone from* SALLY *and she turns off the music:)*

LUCY: *(Out of breath)* You get the idea… It keeps going like that… You think Mom would like it?

(Lights fade.)

6.
The Wake.

(The same a short time later)

(On their way out, LUCY *and* MAY *pick at a few things to eat.)*

IRENIE: Have fun!

MAY: We will.

LUCY: See you guys there!

DAVID: See you after?

LUCY: For a few minutes, Dad.

SUZANNE: They're going to go out with their friends after, David.

DAVID: Where will you be going?

SALLY: *(To* DAVID*)* It doesn't matter.

MAY: *(To* SUZANNE*)* You know which studios?

SUZANNE: F and G.

KATE: Aren't you hungry?

SUZANNE: *(The dress)* You going to wear that out?

LUCY: I want to show my dancers. See what they think. I'll change there.

SALLY: Do you have your masks?

LUCY: We have them.

IRENIE: Does everyone wear them?

LUCY: Not everyone, Irenie. Not here.

IRENIE: I've seen that.

LUCY: And we have our health passes…

SUZANNE: To get in anywhere.

KATE: Where are you going?

SUZANNE: There's the fringe tonight.

LUCY: We have to set up, Kate.

SUZANNE: We have plenty of time. No rush.

LUCY: Kate, I still can't believe Mom thought I wouldn't want the dress…

KATE: I know.

LUCY: See you later. Come on, May.

(MAY and LUCY go.)

(Short pause)

SUZANNE: Dinner.

DAVID: *(A joke)* About time!

SALLY: He's hungry.

SUZANNE: I've made you hungry.

IRENIE: It looks delicious, Suzanne.

KATE: It does.

SALLY: Thank you for doing all of this.

KATE: The girls aren't hungry?

SUZANNE: They're dancing. They'll eat after. We'll do a buffet. *(Then)* What was Rose thinking?

IRENIE: About the dress?

KATE: She got things mixed up. Dates. She called me Alice. I don't know.

IRENIE: Lucy looks great in that dress.

SUZANNE: She really does.

SALLY: I needed that…I needed some dancing. I think we've earned that.

IRENIE: To see dance. And not on Zoom.

DAVID: I've been really looking forward to tomorrow. Even more now.

SALLY: Me too. They seem great, Suzanne… Good work, Thank you.

IRENIE: They really do, Suzanne.

SUZANNE: Everyone, help yourselves. David could you get more wine and cider…?

DAVID: And she looked just like Rose. *(He goes off.)*

SALLY: What can I get you, Kate?

KATE: I'm fine. I can do it.

IRENIE: *(To* SUZANNE*)* It's been a lot of work for you with Lucy. And then with both girls…

SALLY: You hadn't counted on having Lucy for a year and a half.

SUZANNE: I was no longer taking care of my helpless brother… *(A joke)* So I have plenty of time on my hands. You know he never fucking learned to drive. There's a driving school about five doors down the street.

IRENIE: Your brother.

SUZANNE: I drove him everywhere. That was half my life. So I got that time back. I love having them here.

KATE: Does his wife drive?

SUZANNE: I'm sure it was a prerequisite. Maybe the main one…

(As DAVID *returns with wine and cider:)*

IRENIE: I don't know about any of you, but I forgot everything else, everything—watching them dance…

(They will seat themselves and will begin to eat.)

DAVID: Me too. I know. And in this room.

SALLY: *(Repeats)* And in this room, Suzanne.

IRENIE: What do you mean?

SUZANNE: Right… Of course.

KATE: I don't understand either.

DAVID: Sally feels it too. We talked about this last night when we arrived.

SALLY: This was the place to be, Kate.

KATE: What do you mean?

SALLY: This apartment.

IRENIE: You've told me this.

DAVID: This kitchen. There's so much dance history right in this kitchen…

SALLY: Explain that to Kate.

DAVID: Jacques Francois had these conferences. About dance.

KATE: You told me.

DAVID: And we all came—.

IRENIE: I've never been here, Kate.

SALLY: I only got invited because of David.

DAVID: Dancers from all over the world. He held them at the theater in town.

SUZANNE: The Grand. Before there was the Quai.

DAVID: Speaker after speaker—on dance. Dancers. Then after the audience left, Jacques Francois would raise the theater curtain, and there on the stage of this jewel box—a large table beautifully set for a beautiful dinner.

SUZANNE: Very *Fanny and Alexander*.

DAVID: He was always very witty with his toasts. Thanked his sister... *(Bows to* SUZANNE*)*

SALLY: She'd done most of the work.

SUZANNE: That is true.

DAVID: And then Kate, we'd all come back here to this kitchen. People might dance... *(To* IRENIE*)* Trisha. Paul. Sitting right there...

SALLY: *(To* IRENIE*)* Simone. Even Dan one year came from Florida. *(To* KATE*)* If you didn't understand the language someone was speaking, you just got up and gestured and danced. It's how you spoke to each other.

KATE: And Alice?

DAVID: She of course came with Rose...

SALLY: You walk in and it looks like nothing special.

SUZANNE: Thank you...

SALLY: You know what I mean. A floor, some bits of furniture, a few rugs, a sink, a stove... But it's a very special place, Kate. This room.

SUZANNE: It can be, Sally, but not always. Sometimes it can feel just empty... I once saw an exhibit in Paris. About the earliest scientific journeys; drawings of newly discovered plants and species. When the explorers got home, they didn't know what to call where they'd been. They needed to invent a word for this thrilling other place 'out there'.

DAVID: What word did they invent?

SUZANNE: 'Elsewhere.' Lucy and I made a private joke out of it. When we were locked in, we'd sit in here, doing whatever to pass the time, and when either one of us got too bored, we'd whisper— 'elsewhere… elsewhere… '

(Then)

SALLY: It's delicious, Suzanne.

DAVID: It is… It's really good.

KATE: In my guidebook it said there's a street here called—is this true, Suzanne? 'The Promenade on the Edge of the World.'

SUZANNE: By the ruins of the Chateau. You passed it from the train station…

(Then)

KATE: Where did Rose sit?

DAVID: Here. There.

SUZANNE: No one place. She moved around…

SALLY: I remember one time her sitting right here. And Rose, she'd had a drink or two, and she sits with me and says, 'when you told me you were going to marry David…'

(Everyone is interested in this.)

SALLY: I'd told her that like ten years before. We'd now been married for nine years. Now she brings this up. *(Then)* She says, 'I was so worried, Sally, that you weren't clever enough." *(Points)* Right there… We were there.

DAVID: Finish what she said, Sal.

SALLY: 'Clever enough—to make him happy. But I was wrong.'

KATE: Very Rose.

(Then)

SUZANNE: My brother always sat at the head. There. That was his seat.

IRENIE: Suzanne, where does your brother live now?

DAVID: A couple of streets away. You can see their place through Suzanne's back window. We're staying with him and Maria.

SUZANNE: The wife.

DAVID: She has a name…

(Then)

SUZANNE: Speaking of Rose.

DAVID: When have we stopped speaking of Rose?

SUZANNE: She treated him so much better than she ever treated us.

KATE: Your brother?

DAVID: Us…?

SALLY: *(Obviously)* Women.

DAVID: I never saw that.

SALLY: Come on, David.

SUZANNE: She was always looking out for him. We could be starving, sick as dogs…

IRENIE: So true.

SUZANNE: Nothing. No sympathy.

IRENIE: 'Get the fuck on with it.'

SUZANNE: But every single morning, he'd come in and she'd poke my brother in the stomach, *(Voice)* 'What have you had for breakfast?' Or 'Don't buy your breakfast on the way to the subway.' Or 'You—use real butter.' We could be licking our breakfast off the fucking sidewalk and she wouldn't notice.

IRENIE: Very very spoiled.

SUZANNE: I spoiled him too… His wife's probably spoiling him as we speak.

(Then)

DAVID: Suzanne, I don't think Lucy's going to stay in Angers much past her festival. She wants to travel.

SUZANNE: I know. And May's leaving.

SALLY: Kate can't afford any more…

SUZANNE: *(To* KATE*)* Of course you can't.

KATE: I really wish I could.

SUZANNE: I'll miss them.

DAVID: I'm sure.

SALLY: I'd like them both home with us. Lucy's like my own daughter… May now too. I've missed them too.

IRENIE: You're selling your house.

SUZANNE: They've been like sisters to me. What would I have done without them?

IRENIE: Lucy can always stay in New York with me. I think I'm her godmother…I think so. I don't know for sure…Rose wasn't very clear about that.

SALLY: Listen to us… Look, they're not going to want to hang around with us.

IRENIE: Why not?

*(*SUZANNE *smiles.)*

IRENIE: What?

SUZANNE: Lucy told me about a guy she went to school with… His mothers are gay. They were married, but then divorced. Then they each married again. So now he has four mothers.

DAVID: Poor boy.

SUZANNE: She said, nice guy, but whenever he entered a room he always assumed everyone was looking at him… Interested in him. She said he became an actor…

IRENIE: And May…? What is she going to do?

SUZANNE: Go home to her Mom. It's what her Mom wants. She says she needs her help with the motel. She's got money problems…

KATE: What about her dancing?

(Then)

SUZANNE: Kate, I think May did mention something about a friend who was worried she'd gotten her grandmother infected.

DAVID: With Covid?

SUZANNE: It never even occurred to me that she was talking about herself… *(Then)* This was such a gift to May, Kate… Coming to Europe. Being around young dancers… Around dance. And a gift to me.

(They eat.)

IRENIE: Suzanne, this is Kate's first trip to Europe.

SUZANNE: Lucy told me that.

KATE: Rose and I had planned a trip before she got cancer.

SUZANNE: To France?

KATE: Europe. She got me to get a passport.

SUZANNE: And now your first stop is Angers…? So any plans? Anything you want to see?

DAVID: In Angers? What's to see?

KATE: I do. My guidebook says there's a seminary here…?

SUZANNE: I'm not sure….

KATE: And Jews were imprisoned there, sent off from there to the camps…. I read that there's a plaque. I'd like to a take a photo for my brother. He refuses to come to Europe… Rose wanted to take me to Germany. Berlin. She told me, 'It won't heal you. But it's a good thing to do. To face what has been lost.' Today is the second day of Rosh Hashanah.

DAVID: We'll all go with you and look for this plaque…

KATE: Thank you… *(Smiles)* Rose would have liked this.

IRENIE: What?

KATE: You know how she resented being the one with the problem. 'Like I've failed somehow,' she'd say.

DAVID: I know.

KATE: So she'd find this very funny.

SALLY: What?

KATE: Today—or yesterday? Whenever I got on the plane at J F K? I was going through security, and I had to take my shoes off. I was already tired. I hadn't slept. I couldn't sleep. Now I think it's been days. And I take off my shoes. And go right through, and then I can't find my shoes. I'm walking around in my socks and I can't find my shoes. And one of the people who works there—

DAVID: The T S A.

KATE: She comes to me with a very worried look and says, 'Ma'am, are you being accompanied?'

(Laughter)

DAVID: Did you find your shoes?

SALLY: *(Obviously)* Of course she did.

KATE: Rose would have laughed so hard at me. And she had that terrible laugh.

SUZANNE: Oh we know!

(Laughter)

KATE: Scary… *(She reaches for something.)*

IRENIE: What do you— *(Need)*?

KATE: I'm getting my wine glass, Irenie. I'm drinking water too, Sally… Before she got Covid, Rose talked about a dance…

IRENIE: Of course she did.

SALLY: Duh…

KATE: I feel like talking. Is that all right?

IRENIE: Of course.

*(*KATE *pushes her plate away:)*

KATE It's delicious, Suzanne. But I'm not hungry. Thank you. *(Continues)* Rose would close her eyes and just imagine this dance. Visualize it, I guess. She showed me this poem. *(Then)* About a ploughman and his beautiful young wife and she dies. From hundreds of years ago. The ploughman is obviously upset, grieves. He hunts down Death and confronts him, 'how could you do this, sir?' He's very respectful. 'This is so unfair. You didn't know her, but if you did, you'd see how she did not deserve this injustice.' *(Then)* Death argues back, 'hey I'm just doing my job, don't blame me, mister. Now you just get on with your life. I'll see you later.' But the ploughman won't give up, and so they argue back and forth, back and forth. It's beautiful and heartbreaking. And then God intervenes. He's been listening of course, and God says, 'you know I really enjoyed that discussion, guys, the passion, the commitment you both brought to your arguments. But

Ploughman, you must understand one very important thing, and face up to it: 'there is no life without death'.

(Then)

SUZANNE: That's…

KATE: What?

SUZANNE: True…

KATE: At the same time she showed me a book of drawings, called *The Dance of Death.*

IRENIE: *(To* SALLY*)* I remember her showing us that.

KATE: You know she hated mirrors.

SALLY: We know that.

IRENIE: *(Same time)* She really did. Why?

SUZANNE: *(Same time)* Every studio, we had to cover the mirrors. 'Tape up the newspapers!'

KATE: In one of the drawings in this book—death is in a mirror… *(Then)* Another story?

DAVID: Please… You knew her best these last two years.

IRENIE: You did…

SALLY: A Rose story?

KATE: Maybe. On the plane, in the middle of the night, I suddenly think, 'where's my passport?' I don't know why I suddenly thought that, but I get out my purse. It's not there. I push up the tray and it's not in the little seat pocket. Is it under my bag? Fallen on the floor? I check my coat pockets. Have I left it in the Starbuck's at J F K? I remember looking at it then. I hate my picture. *(Then)* I don't know what to do, David. What to say when I get to Paris. I panic. I think I'm crying. And I look down. And on my lap, *my lap*—is my passport… It hadn't been there. I'd stood up, sat down.

It's impossible. But it's there. *(A real question)* How did it get there?

DAVID: Maybe you fell asleep and someone saw it on the floor in the aisle, and saw the photo and set it on your lap.

KATE: I hadn't fallen asleep, David. I couldn't sleep.

IRENIE: You think Rose?

KATE: I don't know, Irenie. When Rose was in the hospital, we discovered that we had had the same dream, the same night. We're in my backyard garden. There's wind and Rose's straw hat blows off—actually it's my hat she was wearing. It was my hat in both of our dreams. We run and chase it. She could run. That's it. That was the dream. Not very special.

SUZANNE: Except it was the same dream.

KATE: Yeh. It was. She sometimes talked to Alice. And sometimes I was Alice.

DAVID: We knew that.

KATE: Once she said to me, "Alice, life doesn't last. Art doesn't last. And it doesn't matter…" When she said this I thought she was being bitter… Angry. But I had misunderstood. It's not that it doesn't matter. It's that it doesn't matter that it doesn't last. *(Then)* Because we are ephemeral, does not mean we don't matter. This pandemic I think taught me that more than anything. Stuck inside. The same routines. Everything became small. And everything small became big. *(Then)* I remembered a story I read somewhere and Rose liked this a lot. A peasant years ago who had never ever left her village. And how today we see such a life as being narrow and without 'experiences', perhaps to be pitied. Or condescended to. But that is not how this story unfolds: because in this story it shows that so much of the world, maybe even all of it, we can find, say, over a meal, or with the simplest of routines, the subtlest of gestures. *(Then)* One more… They're just popping into my head right now. Because I'm tired? Because I'm here?

IRENIE: We've been talking about Rose all day.

KATE: True.

IRENIE: I think that's why I'm here. To talk about Rose.

KATE: Right. *(Then)* She told me about a play she saw. Somewhere. The characters are all sitting around a table. *(She touches the table.)* The actors doing this play are all deaf. They act with sign language. This big table it goes right to the seats. So that at one end the audience begins. The line between the actors and the audience is blurred. *(Then)* In the play, it's one of the character's birthday and she's with her sisters and brother and friends. Someone gives her a top, a spinning top, as a present. She pumps it on the table, she lets go, and the top spins. One by one the characters put their chins or their cheeks or their foreheads down against this table—so they can feel its vibration. Rose said, we knew what they were all feeling, without a word being said. And then she noticed a man in the audience at the end of this table, put his head down to feel it too. He wants to share in what the characters are feeling… He wants to be at that table too… I am tired…

(Short pause)

DAVID: Rose, God bless you. Who needs wine…?

(No one needs more wine.)

KATE: And for everyone who's died, David…

(They raise their glasses.)

(A long moment of silence)

(Lights fade.)

7.
Moving On.

(The same, a short time later. The dinner is over.)

*(*SUZANNE *and* DAVID *stand and have begun to pick up the plates. They will scrape them into the garbage.)*

(Church bells from the nearby church as:)

IRENIE: What time is it?

KATE: *(A joke)* In Rhinebeck?

SUZANNE: Almost eight thirty. We should go. Their slot's soon. But they're probably running late. They always do.

DAVID: It's France…

IRENIE: That was so great, Suzanne. Thank you.

DAVID: It really was….

SALLY: Can we have coffee?

DAVID: When we get back, Sally.

SUZANNE: We'll buy coffee there. That'll be open… And all of you, when you see him, tell my brother he's missed a wonderful Italian dinner.

DAVID: We'll tell him, Suzanne.

SUZANNE: His new wife is Italian. And she's a terrible cook. He told me this himself. Then he got worried, *(His voice)* 'Suzanne, don't tell her I said that. Please!'

IRENIE: Have you told her?

*(*SALLY *has started to pick up.)*

SUZANNE: Not yet. Leave it, Sally. I'll do the dishes later. *(To* SALLY*)* Here, put this *(The lasagna)* in the fridge.

*(*SALLY *will go off to the fridge.)*

SUZANNE: David, just put those *(Plates)* in the sink. Finish your wine…

DAVID: We can bring down the garbage with us.

(SUZANNE sets the antipasto dishes on a tray.)

SUZANNE: Let's do that. Good idea. It can start to smell…Irenie, when he told me about getting married, he did it on the phone. From his office.

IRENIE: He was scared…

SUZANNE: I'd given up two serious relationships, both men insisted I move out of here… *(She heads for the kitchen.)*

SALLY: *(Passing SUZANNE)* Suzanne, can I borrow a sweater? I saw one in the living room…

SUZANNE: Take what you need, Sal…

(SALLY heads for the living room.)

(DAVID, KATE and IRENIE alone:)

DAVID: Long day?

KATE: David, maybe I shouldn't go to the fringe with you tonight. I feel tired. It just hit me. It has been a long day. I think I'm ready to sleep now.

DAVID: You haven't slept for like a day and a half.

KATE: Has it been that long? You think the girls will be upset if I don't go?

DAVID: I know they won't, Kate. They'll understand. It means so much to them that you're here.

KATE: Thank you for saying that.

IRENIE: The real thing's tomorrow. And you'll be there.

DAVID: You want to go bed?

KATE: I think so. In a little while.

IRENIE: And try to sleep late. You'll probably wake up early. I always do my first day… Your body gets confused.

KATE: Rose should have been here… With all of you. And watching her daughter dance. I'm not Rose…

DAVID: You made a very long trip to get here, Kate. I know it wasn't easy.

KATE: I'm vaccinated.

DAVID: I didn't mean that. And you know it.

*(*SUZANNE *returns.)*

IRENIE: *(To* SUZANNE*)* Kate's going to stay here. She's tired.

SUZANNE: I think that's a good idea. Of course you are. My god… You want to go to bed?

KATE: Not quite yet. Very soon. You all go. And give me a full report.

DAVID: We'll do that.

SUZANNE: Your bed's very very comfortable. My brother made sure of that. He is so damned spoiled.

KATE: Sounds good.

IRENIE: Suzanne, Sally told me that they do, like, an open mic in the fringe. But for dance. I was thinking why don't I put my name down…

*(*SALLY *returns with the sweater.)*

DAVID: Tonight?

SUZANNE: Why not?

SALLY: *(About the sweater)* Thank you, Suzanne.

SUZANNE: Kate's not coming. She's too tired.

SALLY: I was going to suggest that.

KATE: I think I can sleep now, Sally.

SALLY: Good.

SUZANNE: There are extra blankets in your closet… It can get a little cold at night. And we keep the windows open…

DAVID: Sally, Irenie's thinking of dancing tonight in the fringe.

SALLY: What? You just ate.

IRENIE: I've been working on a dance in my apartment, Sal.

SALLY: What are you talking about?

IRENIE: My dog loved it.

SALLY: You're going to dance in their fringe?

IRENIE: If I'm allowed. If I'm picked.

SALLY: *(To* DAVID*)* I don't believe this.

IRENIE: I call my dance: 'we dance differently at sixty.' Not a lot of fast movements. So I can do it on a full stomach.

KATE: That's funny.

SALLY: She's not serious?

DAVID: I don't know…

KATE: Rose would sometimes say things that I'd write down.

IRENIE: Like what?

KATE: "We tell ourselves, 'there are things we can't forgive ourselves for.' But then we do, all the time…"

DAVID: She said that?

SUZANNE: Maybe share that with May sometime.

KATE: Good idea. And Irenie, I thought of this earlier.

IRENIE: What?

KATE: One day she said: "I don't know, Kate. I think I used to know."

(They laugh.)

KATE: I laughed too. She didn't think it was funny. Now you go. I'm fine. You're going to be late. Don't disappoint the girls…

(Then)

IRENIE: Kate, don't even think about doing any dishes.

KATE: I won't. I promise. I'm going to go to bed…

SUZANNE: So who's watching your dog, Irenie?

(As they get up:)

IRENIE: A girlfriend with a new puppy. She says he's really happy. We needed some time apart.

SALLY: David, leave it.

DAVID: I'm just getting the garbage… Kate, you need anything? You going to be all right?

KATE: That's a big question. *(She smiles.)* I'm fine. Have fun. And give me a full report in the morning.

SUZANNE: We will.

IRENIE: Goodnight, Kate.

DAVID: Goodnight. *(With the garbage, to* SALLY*)* I'll take this out. *(He goes.)*

SALLY: Goodnight. Everyone have their masks?

IRENIE: Mine's in my jacket.

SUZANNE: And our health passes… You think it's over and then… Goodnight.

KATE: Goodnight everyone… Have fun.

SUZANNE: I have hand sanitizer in my purse.

IRENIE: With Vitamin E?

SUZANNE: Yeh.

SALLY: *(Over this)* I keep an extra mask in my pocket…

IRENIE: I do too…

SALLY: *(Over this)* In case I want to double mask…

SUZANNE: *(Leaving)* I really want to see Irenie dance…

(They are gone.)

*(*KATE *is alone.)*

(She looks over the room as, quietly:)

(Music: Katie Herzig's Lost and Found.*)*

*(*KATE *finds her water glass.)*

(She will go to the sink and get water.)

(Sipping her water, she looks around the room.)

(She picks up her bag, and begins to leave.)

(And she is off to bed.)

(Then:)

(Blackout)

END OF PLAY

NOTE

I consulted numerous books, articles, essays, newspapers, journals while researching WHAT HAPPENED?: THE MICHAELS ABROAD. These are the most important about dance: *UBU: Scenes d'Europe, No 52/52: 'La danse en questions'* with articles by Chantal Aubry & Fabienne Arvers; Laurence Louppe; Philippe Noisette; and interviews with Boris Charmatz by Pascale Gateau; Myriam Gourfink by Maia Bouteillet; Francois Verret by Joelle Gayot; Herman Diephuis by Pascale Gateau; Robyn Orlin, Daniel Linehan, Mathilde, Abou Lagraa all by Chantal Boiron. *Europe Dancing: Perspectives on Theatre dance and Cultural Identity*, edited by Andree Grau and Stephanie Jordon, especially Georgianna Gore and Laurence Louppe's essay, with Wilfride Piollet, 'France, Effervescence and tradition in French Dance.' Sally Baines' three brilliant books: *Terpsichore in Sneakers, Democracy's Body: Judson Dance Theater,* and *Dancing Women: Female Bodies on Stage*; Yvonne Rainer's *Feelings Are Facts: A Life*; Twyla Tharp's *Push Comes To Shove: An Autobiography*; Paul Taylor's *Private Domain: An Autobiography*; Janice Ross' *Anna Halprin: Experience As Dance*; Connie Kreemer's *Further Steps: Fifteen Choreographers of Modern Dance*; *Merce Cunningham Dancing in Space and Time*, edited by Richard Kostelanetz; Marion Meyer's *Pina Bausch: The Biography*; *Dance: Documents of Contemporary Art*, edited by Andre Lepecki; *The Vision of Modern Dance*, edited by Jean Morrison Brown; *Contemporary Dance: An Anthology of Lectures, Interviews and Essays*, edited by Anne Livet, Wendy Perron's *Through the Eyes of a Dancer*; Roslyn Sulcas' 'At Lyon Biennale,' New York Times, Sept. 24, 2018; David Velasco's description in *Artforum* of the last performances of the Merce Cunningham Company.

Other helpful books that I consulted: Johannnes von Saaz's *Death and the Ploughman* (translated by Michael West), Hans Holbein's *The Dance of Death* (commentary by Ulnka Rublack, Penguin Books); *The Guide to Angers*, forward by Jerome Clement (Editions du Patrimoine, 2013); Oliver Sacks' *Gratitude*.

The dances credited to Lucy and Rose are based upon dances by Dan Wagoner.

I am indebted to the Jerome Robbins Collection at the Performing Arts Library at Lincoln Center and Gwyneth Jones for her copy of the videos of Dan Wagoner's dances.

WHAT HAPPENED?: THE MICHAELS ABROAD is the second of a two-play series. This series is part of a group called *The Rhinebeck Panorama*, which also includes the four-play series, *The Apple Family*, a trilogy of Zoom plays about the Apple family, and the three-play series, *The Gabriels*.

R.N.

www.ingramcontent.com/pod-product-compliance
Lightning Source LLC
LaVergne TN
LVHW010630100826
845148LV00014B/3176

* 9 7 8 0 8 8 1 4 5 9 1 5 9 *